Kids' Birthday Cakes

igloobooks

Published in 2016
by Igloo Books Ltd
Cottage Farm
Sywell
NN6 0BJ
www.igloobooks.com

Food photography and recipe development:
© Stockfood, The Food Media Agency

Except for the following images:
50, 81, 85, 93 © Clive Bozzard-Hill / Getty Images, 26 © Will Heap / Getty Images
28 © Mark Kelly / Getty Images, 53 © Sol de Zuasnabar Brebbia / Getty Images
8, 9, 11, 25, 27, 34, 37, 41, 45, 74, 77, 90 © iStock / Getty Images

Cover Images: Clive Bozzard-Hill / © Getty Images

All other non-recipe images: © iStock / Getty Images

LEO002 0616
2 4 6 8 10 9 7 5 3 1
ISBN 978-1-78440-241-9

Cover designed by Nicholas Gage
Interiors designed by Stephen Jorgensen
Edited by Caroline Icke

Printed and manufactured in China

Contents

Introduction

A child's birthday can only mean one thing – cake! Choosing a birthday cake is an exciting task for kids. Is this the year for an amazing knight's castle, or perhaps a spectacular circus? What about a giant ladybird, or a creepy crawly spider? Make blowing out the candles extra special this year with Kids' Birthday Cakes, a guide to making unforgettable cakes for children.

Whether you're baking for boys or girls, you'll find a huge range of cakes to cater for kids of all ages, from pirate ships and pretty princesses to green dinosaurs and exploding volcanoes. There's even a selection of cupcakes and cake pops, with plenty of fun designs to choose from.

This exciting new book is split into three chapters: Cake Basics, Birthday Cakes and Cupcakes and Cake Pops. Cake Basics includes a number of basic recipes, including popular sponges, frosting and toppings. These will be referred to throughout the book, so it's a good idea to get to know these staples.

Birthday Cakes is where you'll find the special cakes! These recipes take basic sponge cakes and transform them into tasty show-stoppers! A good tip is to read the entire recipe before you start, so you know exactly what you need to bake and prepare beforehand. The prep and cook time with each recipe accounts for the entire cake-making process, including the basic cake and any toppings. You can buy some ready-made ingredients (such as fondant icing), if you want to speed up the cake-making process.

Cupcakes and Cake Pops is a chapter dedicated to smaller cakes, which make wonderful projects to ease beginners into the art of cake decorating. They may be small, but they go down a treat with both kids and grown-ups!

Cake decorating can require a bit of preparation, so over the next few pages you'll find the basic tools you'll need to get started. Plus, discover party tips towards the end of the book, so you can throw an unforgettable party for your kids.

Don't forget to make a wish!

Cake baker's tool box

Cake decorating is a popular craft. You'll notice a wide range of tools available on the market that differ from your basic baking tools.

The recipes in this book use as few specialist tools as possible, but there are a few essentials that you might want to consider as you attempt more elaborate cakes.

Cake boards

Cake boards are the ideal base for your cake, providing a stable and hygienic surface for the finished cake to sit on. It's a good idea to choose a slightly larger board than your cake, especially if you want to decorate the base of the cake, too.

Cake tins

Cake tins are essential for cake baking, so it's worth investing in a few different sizes. In addition to the basic shapes, you can buy plenty of customized tins that are perfect for baking number or animal shapes.

Cutters

Cutters come in a range of shapes and sizes, allowing you to cut precise shapes. You can buy simple cutters such as circles and stars, or novelty shapes that help you create much more intricate designs. It's worth investing in a range of cutters and building up a collection over time.

Fondant rolling pins

Non-stick rolling pins are ideal for fondant work and are available in a variety of sizes to help you evenly roll larger pieces of fondant.

Fondant tools

Specialist shops supply a wide range of tools for use with fondant, each creating a different effect. These include shaped moulds, border cutters, modelling tools and crimpers, such as the below:

Ball tool: a spherical tool used to make indents in leaves, flowers and petals.

Bone tool: ideal for thinning, smoothing and creating frills.

Scriber tool: ideal for marking outlines and inscribing designs onto cake sides, fondant, royal icing and chocolate.

Serrated and tapered cone tool: used to make cone-shaped indents.

You can create most effects using utensils that you already own, if you don't want to splash out on the collection.

Greaseproof paper

This is an essential addition to a baker's kitchen and is most often used to line cake tins for easy-release cakes. You can also use greaseproof paper to make disposable piping bags, or as a non-stick surface for sugar and fondant work.

Icing smoothers

These are essential for fondant work, and will help to achieve a professional, smooth finish to fondant-covered cakes, or marzipan. They are sometimes called 'cake polishers'.

Kitchen knives

A good set of knives is essential for any kitchen, so you might find that you have something suitable already. Some recipes in this book refer to a serrated knife and/or a paring knife. A serrated knife has a scalloped, saw-like edge that is useful for trimming cakes, whereas a paring knife is small with a plain edge, and can be used for creating finer details.

Kitchen thermometer

This is most useful for sugar work, when the heating temperatures are precise (and very hot!). They're inexpensive and a useful tool for cooking and baking.

Measuring tools

Tape measures, rulers and rolling guides are useful for cake decorating, and the good news is that you probably already have one or more of these in the house! Accurate measurements can be the difference between a cake success and a mess, so these are handy little tools to have around.

Paintbrushes

A clean set of paintbrushes is essential for cake decorating and can be used for painting directly onto iced cakes. They're also handy for sticking decorations to cakes and manipulating fondant. Always make sure you clean your brushes thoroughly after use to prevent them from clogging and keep them for kitchen use only!

Palette knife and angled spatulas

A staple in any kitchen, palette knives are useful for smoothing fillings and toppings onto cakes. You'll only need one of these, although there are different sizes available if you feel you need more.

Piping bags and nozzles

Whilst you can make disposable piping bags from greaseproof paper, a selection of washable bags with a range of nozzles will be more effective for cake decorating. Different nozzles create different effects and control how much icing is pushed through. Start with a simple selection and build up your collection as you become more adept at piping. Piping bags and nozzles are extremely versatile, allowing you to create large and small details.

Revolving cake stand

Revolving cake stands make the decorating process much easier, allowing you to rotate the cake around freely while you work. They're not essential for beginners, but are a useful purchase if you plan to ice a lot of cakes.

Cake
basics

Vanilla sponge cake

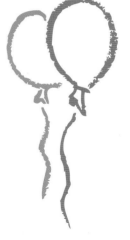

Serves: 8 Prep and cook time: 55 minutes

Ingredients

For the sponge:
225 g / 8 oz / 1 cup unsalted butter, softened
225 g / 8 oz / 1 cup caster (superfine) sugar
4 medium eggs, beaten
2 tsp vanilla extract
225 g / 8 oz / 1 ½ cups self-raising flour, sifted
2 tbsp cornflour (cornstarch)
1-2 tbsp whole milk

Method

1. Preheat the oven to 170°C (150°C fan) / 325F / gas 3. Grease and line the base of two 20 cm (8 in) cake tins with greaseproof paper.

2. Cream together the butter and sugar in a large mixing bowl until pale and fluffy. Beat in the eggs a little at a time, then beat in the vanilla extract.

3. Fold in the flour, cornflour and milk until the batter is smooth and even. Divide between the two cake tins and tap them gently on a work surface to settle the batter.

4. Bake for 30-40 minutes until golden, risen and springy to the touch. A cake tester should come out clean from their centres. Remove to a wire rack to cool.

Chocolate sponge

Serves: 8 Prep and cook time: 50 minutes

Ingredients

150 g / 5 oz / ⅔ cup unsalted
    butter, softened
150 g / 5 oz / ⅔ cup golden caster
    (superfine) sugar
110 g / 4 oz / ⅔ cup self-raising
    flour, sifted
55 g / 2 oz / ⅓ cup good-quality
    cocoa powder
a pinch of salt
3 medium eggs

Method

1. Preheat the oven to 180°C (160°C fan) / 350F / gas 4. Grease and line a 20 cm (8 in) springform cake tin.

2. Cream together the butter and sugar in a large mixing bowl for 2-3 minutes until pale and fluffy.

3. Mix together the flour, cocoa powder and salt in a separate bowl. Add one-third to the creamed butter with 1 egg, then beat well.

4. Add half of the remaining flour mixture with another egg and beat well. Add the rest of the flour mixture with the last egg and beat until you have a smooth, even batter.

5. Spoon into the prepared tin and tap gently on a work surface to settle the batter. Bake for 20-25 minutes until risen and springy to the touch. Remove to a wire rack to cool.

Fruit cake

Serves: 10 Prep and cook time: 2 hours 45 minutes

Ingredients

175 g / 6 oz / ¾ cup unsalted
   butter, softened
175 g / 6 oz / 1 cup soft light
   brown sugar
1 orange, zested
3 tbsp apricot jam (jelly)
3 medium eggs, beaten
225 g / 8 oz / 1 ½ cups plain
   (all-purpose) flour
1 tsp baking powder
75 g / 2 ½ oz / ¾ cup ground
   almonds
2 tbsp whole milk
450 g / 1 lb / 3 cups mixed dried
   fruits: sultanas, raisins, currants
100 g / 3 ½ oz / ⅔ cup glacé
   cherries, chopped

Method

1. Preheat the oven to 170°C (150°C fan) / 325F / gas 3.
   Grease and line the base of a 20 cm (8 in) springform cake
   tin with greaseproof paper.

2. Cream together the butter and sugar in a large mixing bowl
   for 2–3 minutes until pale and fluffy. Briefly beat in the orange
   zest and apricot jam.

3. Beat in the eggs, little by little, until incorporated. Fold through the
   flour, baking powder, ground almonds and milk.

4. Stir in the mixed dried fruits and glacé cherries, then spoon
   the batter into the prepared tin and smooth the top with a spatula
   dipped in water.

5. Bake for 1 hour 45 minutes–2 hours 15 minutes until golden on
   top and a cake tester comes out almost clean from its centre;
   there should be just a few crumbs on the tester.

6. Remove to a wire rack to cool completely. Turn out when ready
   and decorate with ribbon if you're not decorating the cake.

Carrot cake

Serves: 10 Prep and cook time: 1 hour 15 minutes

Ingredients

2 large eggs
125 ml / 4 ½ fl. oz / ½ cup
    sunflower oil
3 tbsp honey
225 g / 8 oz / 2 cups plain
    (all-purpose) flour
½ tsp bicarbonate of (baking) soda
½ tsp baking powder
1 tsp mixed spice
125 g / 4 ½ oz courgettes
    (zucchinis), grated and drained
125 g / 4 ½ oz carrots, grated
1 large banana, chopped

Method

1. Preheat the oven to 180°C (160°C fan) 350F gas 4. Grease and line the base of a 23 cm (9 in) cake tin with greaseproof paper.

2. Beat together the eggs, oil and honey in a mixing bowl.

3. Sift in the flour, bicarbonate of soda, baking powder and spice.

4. Stir in the courgettes, carrots and banana until blended.

5. Pour into the tin and bake for 40–50 minutes until a cake tester comes out clean. Cool in the tin for 10 minutes, then turn out onto a wire rack to cool completely.

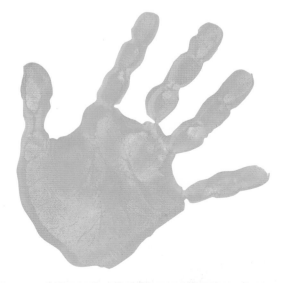

Lemon cake

Ingredients

4 medium eggs, separated
2 tbsp lemon zest
½ tsp lemon extract
110 g / 4 oz / ½ cup caster
   (superfine) sugar
175 g / 6 oz / 1⅔ cups ground
   almonds
1 tsp baking powder
a pinch of salt
1 tsp white vinegar
2 tbsp icing (confectioners') sugar,
   for dusting

Method

1. Preheat the oven to 170°C (150°C fan) / 325F / gas 3 and grease and line the base of a 20 cm (8 in) springform cake tin with greaseproof paper.

2. Beat together the egg yolks, lemon zest, lemon extract and half the sugar in a mixing bowl for 2-3 minutes until thick and pale.

3. Add the ground almonds and baking powder to the mixture, stirring well to incorporate.

4. Beat the egg whites in a clean, oil-free bowl until frothy, then add the salt and vinegar and continue to beat until softly peaked.

5. Continue to beat the whites, adding the remaining sugar 1 tbsp at a time until thick and glossy. Fold the egg whites into the ground almond mixture.

6. Spoon the batter into the prepared tin, spreading it evenly with the back of a tablespoon. Bake for 30-40 minutes until golden and risen on top.

7. Remove to a wire rack to cool. Once cool, turn out and dust with icing sugar if you're not decorating the cake.

Cake basics

Vanilla cupcakes

Serves: 12 Prep and cook time: 40 minutes

Ingredients

225 g / 8 oz / 1 ½ cups plain
  (all-purpose) flour, sifted
1 ½ tsp baking powder
¼ tsp salt
2 large eggs
175 g / 6 oz / ¾ cup caster
  (superfine) sugar
175 g / 6 oz / ¾ cup unsalted
  butter, melted
1 ½ tsp vanilla extract
120 ml / 4 fl. oz / ½ cup milk

Method

1. Preheat the oven to 180°C (160°C fan) / 350F / gas 4 and line
   a 12-hole cupcake tin with cases.

2. Stir together the flour, baking powder and salt in a large mixing
   bowl, then set aside.

3. Beat together the eggs and sugar in a separate mixing bowl for
   2-3 minutes until pale and frothy.

4. Incorporate the melted butter in a slow, steady stream, beating
   continuously. Add the vanilla extract and beat again briefly.

5. Fold through half of the flour mixture, then mix in the milk.
   Fold in the rest of the flour mixture, taking care not to over-mix
   the batter.

6. Divide the batter between the cases and rap the tin lightly to settle
   the batter. Bake for 18-22 minutes until golden and risen. Remove
   to a wire rack to cool.

Buttercream

Makes: 500 g / 1 lb 2 oz Prep time: 15 minutes

Ingredients

110 g / 4 oz / ½ cup butter,
    softened
½ tsp vanilla extract
400 g / 14 oz / 3 ½ cups icing
    (confectioners') sugar
3-4 tbsp whole milk

Method

1. Beat together the butter and vanilla extract in a large
   mixing bowl until creamy.

2. Beat in the icing sugar, one-quarter at a time, until fully
   incorporated.

3. Beat in the milk 1 tbsp at a time until you reach the
   desired consistency. Cover and chill briefly before using.

Cream cheese icing

Makes: 500 g / 1 lb 2 oz Prep time: 15 minutes

Ingredients

275 g / 10 oz / 1 ¼ cups cream cheese, softened
55 g / 2 oz / ¼ cup butter, softened
1 tsp vanilla extract
175 g / 6 oz / 1 ½ cups icing (confectioners') sugar

Method

1. Beat together the cream cheese, butter and vanilla extract in a large mixing bowl until soft and creamy.

2. Beat in the icing sugar in three additions until fully incorporated. Cover and chill until ready to use.

Royal icing

Makes: 300 g / 10 oz Prep time: 20 minutes

Ingredients

1 ½ tsp lemon juice
250 g / 8 oz / 2 cups royal icing
   (confectioners') sugar, sifted

Method

1. Beat together the lemon juice, royal icing sugar and a little hot water on a low speed until combined and smooth. The icing should be of a thick spreadable consistency.

2. If not using immediately, cover the surface of the icing with an oiled piece of cling film to prevent drying out.

Fondant icing

Makes: 1 kg / 2 lb 2 oz Prep time: 20 minutes

Ingredients

900 g / 2 lb / 7 ¼ cups icing
    (confectioners') sugar, sifted,
    plus extra if needed
55 ml / 2 fl. oz / ¼ cup water
1 tbsp gelatin powder
120 g / 4 oz / ½ cup liquid glucose
1 ½ tbsp glycerine

Method

1. Place the icing sugar in a large mixing bowl and make a well in the centre.

2. Place the water in a small saucepan and sprinkle over the gelatin. Leave it to soften for 5 minutes, then warm the mixture over a low heat, stirring until clear. Remove the saucepan from the heat and stir in the liquid glucose and glycerine.

3. Slowly whisk the liquid glucose mixture into the icing sugar, mixing until blended and a rough ball of fondant forms.

4. Gently knead the fondant, adding a little more icing sugar if sticky, and form into a ball. Wrap in cling film and store at room temperature overnight before using for best results. Do not chill.

Chocolate ganache

Makes: 500 g / 1 lb 2 oz Prep time: 10 minutes

Ingredients

250 g / 9 oz / 1 ⅔ cups dark
   chocolate, 70% cocoa solids,
   chopped
250 ml / 9 fl. oz / 1 cup double
   (heavy) cream
1 tbsp butter, diced

Method

1. Place the chocolate in a heatproof bowl and set aside.

2. Warm the cream in a saucepan set over a moderate heat until
   boiling. Remove from the heat and pour over the chocolate.

3. Leave for 1 minute, then whisk until smooth. Whisk in the butter
   until shiny and smooth.

4. Let the ganache cool and thicken before using.

White choc icing

Makes: 750 g / 1 lb 10 oz Prep time: 20 minutes

Ingredients

175 g / 6 oz / 1 ¼ cups good-quality white chocolate, chopped

225 g / 8 oz / 1 cup unsalted butter, softened

250 g / 9 oz / 2 cups icing (confectioners') sugar, sifted

55 ml / 2 fl. oz / ¼ cup double (heavy) cream

¼ tsp vanilla extract

Method

1. Place the chocolate in a microwaveable bowl and microwave on high in 30-second increments, stirring in between, until melted. Set aside to cool.

2. Cream together the butter and icing sugar in a large mixing bowl for 2-3 minutes until pale and fluffy.

3. Gradually beat in the cream in a slow, steady stream until fully incorporated. Fold through the melted white chocolate and vanilla extract.

4. Beat the icing for 2-3 minutes until fluffy. Cover and chill if not using immediately.

Farmyard carousel cake

Serves: 12 Prep and cook time: 3 hours

Ingredients

For the cake:
2 x vanilla sponge cakes (see page 15)
110 g / 4 oz / ½ cup apricot jam (jelly), warmed

To decorate:
225 g / 8 oz / 1 cup prepared buttercream (see page 26)
200 g / 7 oz yellow fondant icing
150 g / 5 oz red fondant icing
100 g / 4 oz blue fondant icing
300 g / 10 oz green fondant icing
100 g / 4 oz brown fondant icing (see page 29 for fondant icing recipe)
assorted natural food colouring: yellow, red, green, blue, white, grey, brown, black
fondant animal figures
cornflour (cornstarch), for dusting
short cake pole

Method

1. Remove the top half of one sponge with a serrated bread knife. Brush the top with jam. Roll out the yellow fondant, then drape over the top half of the sponge and smooth. Cut the remaining yellow fondant into a serrated strip, flowers and half a sun.

2. Roll out the red fondant to 0.5 cm (¼ in) thickness and cut 11 triangular strips. Dampen them with water using a paintbrush and attach to the yellow sponge to make the top of the carousel. Roll some of the excess into a ball, attach it to the top, then attach the reserved yellow strip to the bottom. Shape any remaining red fondant into flowers and set aside.

3. Spread the top of the uncut sponge with a layer of buttercream. Stack the unused half sponge on top, then cover the whole cake with more buttercream. Roll out the blue fondant and drape over the cake, stopping halfway down the sides. Use white food colouring to paint clouds onto the blue icing and attach the sun.

4. Roll out the green fondant and cut a 30 cm (12 in) round, using a serrated edge, then sit on a cake stand. Re-roll the remaining fondant, cut wide strips and attach to the bottom of the cake under the blue fondant. Lift the cake onto the stand.

5. Gather the remaining green fondant and re-roll into a 25 cm (10 in) round, then snip the edge with scissors to look like grass. Brush the top of the cake with water and lift the icing on top, turning up the border to sit flush with the edge of the cake. Shape another strip of green fondant into grass and set aside.

6. Roll out the brown fondant and cut into strips, then shape into gates and attach to the cake. Use a paring knife to add detail. Shape more green fondant into grass and attach. Slide the top of the carousel onto the cake pole, then slide the pole through the centre of the bottom tier. Arrange the reserved grass around the base of the pole. Position the fondant animals under the carousel along with any fondant flowers.

Octopus cake

Serves: 12 Prep and cook time: 3 hours

Ingredients

For the cake:
2 x quantity vanilla sponge cake
  batter, unbaked (see page 15)
225 g / 8 oz / 1 cup apricot jam
  (jelly), warmed

To decorate:
1 kg / 2 lb 2 oz / 4 ½ cups white
  fondant icing (see page 29)
assorted natural food colouring:
  blue, orange, green, red, yellow,
  grey, black
cornflour (cornstarch), for dusting

Method

1. Divide the cake batter between two lined 18 cm (7 in) and two lined 23 cm (9 in) cake tins. Bake until a cake tester comes out clean, then turn out and level the tops using a serrated knife.

2. Brush the tops with apricot jam and stack the respective sponges on top of each other. Colour 150 g / 5 oz of the fondant with blue colouring, then roll out to 1 cm (½ in) thickness and drape over the smaller cake, smoothing down the top and sides. Repeat this process, using 200 g / 7 oz of coloured fondant for the larger cake. Stack the smaller cake on top of the larger cake.

3. Colour 200 g / 7 oz of the remaining fondant with a little orange colouring and knead until pliable. Shape the fondant into an octopus and sit on top of the cake, draping the legs over the edge and down the sides of the smaller cake.

4. Colour 250 g / 9 oz of the remaining fondant with green colouring and roll out on a work surface dusted with cornflour. Use a stencil cutter to cut out coral shapes and attach them to the cake using a damp paintbrush. Cut one long strip of fondant to run around the base of the cake, attaching it with a little water from the paintbrush. Use a paring knife to add detail.

5. Divide the remaining fondant into five and colour each red, yellow, grey and orange, leaving the last fifth white. Roll out the red and yellow fondant and cut out starfish and shell shapes. Attach them to the cake, reserving the leftover fondant.

6. Use the grey fondant to make rocks and place them around the base of the cake. Shape the remaining red and orange fondant into coral, then place them around the cake.

7. Roll out the white fondant to 0.5 cm (½ in) thickness and cut out rings and various circles. Attach to the cake as bubbles, reserving two larger circles for the octopus eyes. Dab on pupils with a little black colouring. Shape any remaining fondant into sea shells or vegetation and place on the cake before presenting.

Chocolate hedgehog

Serves: 8 Prep and cook time: 1 hour 15 minutes

Ingredients

For the cake:
1 x vanilla sponge cake (see
page 15)

For the ganache:
400 g / 14 oz / 1 ¾ cups prepared
chocolate ganache (see page 30)
55 g / 2 oz / ¼ cup unsalted butter,
very soft

To decorate:
40-45 chocolate fingers
2 blueberries
1 glacé cherry

Method

1. Trim the vanilla sponges into two ovals, one larger than the other. Stack the sponges on top of each other and trim the edge of the cake into the shape of a hedgehog, using a serrated knife to create a smooth edge.

2. Place the chocolate ganache and butter in a bowl and beat thoroughly until combined.

3. Spread the ganache over the hedgehog body with a spatula and use the tines of a fork to rake through the ganache to create a spiked effect. Leave to set for 30 minutes.

4. Poke the chocolate fingers into the cake as spines, then use the blueberries for eyes and the cherry for a nose.

Ladybird cake

Serves: 12 Prep and cook time: 3 hours

Ingredients

For the cake:
1 x quantity vanilla sponge cake
   batter, unbaked (see page 15)
450 g / 1 lb / 2 cups prepared
   buttercream (see page 26)

To decorate:
400 g / 14 oz green fondant icing
400 g / 14 oz red fondant icing
300 g / 10 oz black fondant icing
250 g / 9 oz yellow fondant icing
100 g / 4 oz white fondant icing
100 g / 4 oz dark green fondant
   icing (see page 29 for fondant
   recipe)
assorted natural food colouring:
   pink, black
cornflour (cornstarch), for dusting
5 cocktail sticks

Method

1. Divide the cake batter between three lined 20 cm (8 in) cake tins and one deep, lined 15 cm (6 in) cake tin. Bake until a cake tester comes out clean from their centres.

2. Once cool, turn out and cut an angled section away from the top of the 15 cm (6 in) cake and a shallow angle from one of the larger sponges. Level the two remaining 20 cm (8 in) cakes with a serrated knife and cover with a layer of buttercream. Stack the 20 cm (8 in) cakes with the angled one on top, then cover the whole thing in a layer of buttercream.

3. Roll out the green fondant to 1 cm (½ in) thickness and drape over the stacked 20 cm (8 in) cake, smoothing the top and sides. Trim the excess and re-roll. Sit the angled 15 cm (6 in) cake on top of the larger cake and cover with a layer of buttercream. Drape the fondant over it, smooth evenly and trim any excess.

4. Shape half of the red fondant into the body of a large ladybird. Divide the remaining red fondant into two sizes of smaller ladybird. Use a little white fondant and the black fondant to make the heads, spots and antennas for the ladybirds.

5. Roll two-thirds of the yellow icing into balls and arrange around the base of the top tier. Roll out the remaining yellow fondant and shape into a ribbon and bow. Attach to the base of the cake. Collect any scrap yellow fondant and shape into the centres for 10-12 flowers. Cut out petal shapes out of the white fondant and arrange the petals and flower centres on the side of the cake.

6. Roll out the dark green fondant and cut out leaves, then attach to the sides of the cake and detail with a paring knife.

7. Attach some smaller ladybirds to the cake. Place the rest on the cocktail sticks and insert them next to the yellow balls. Colour any leftover white fondant a light shade pink and shape into dimples for the ladybird on top. Use a little black colouring to paint on detailing where appropriate on the ladybirds.

Pigs in a mud bath

Serves: 8 Prep and cook time: 1 hour 30 minutes

Ingredients

For the cake:
1 x chocolate sponge cake (see page 16)

For the ganache:
200 g / 7 oz / 1 ⅓ cups dark chocolate, chopped
175 ml / 6 fl. oz / ¾ cup double (heavy) cream

To decorate:
44-46 chocolate wafer fingers
250 g / 9 oz / 1 cup pink fondant icing (see page 29)
2 cocktail umbrellas

Method

1. Level the top of the chocolate cake using a serrated knife.

2. Place the chocolate in a heatproof bowl. Heat the cream in a saucepan until it reaches boiling point, then remove from the heat and pour over the chocolate.

3. Leave for 1 minute, then stir the chocolate and cream until melted and smooth. Leave to cool for 10 minutes until thickened.

4. Once thickened, spread over the top and sides of the cake. Stick the chocolate wafer fingers, standing upright, against the side of the cake.

5. Divide the fondant into pieces and shape into pig parts using your hands. Use a cake tester to poke holes for the eyes and noses. Place the pigs on top of the ganache and use a knife to make any final decorations. Garnish with the cocktail umbrellas.

In the wild cake

Serves: 12 Prep and cook time: 2 hours 30 minutes

Ingredients

For the cake:
2 x vanilla sponge cakes (see page 15)
110 g / 4 oz / ½ cup apricot jam (jelly), warmed

To decorate:
900 g / 2 lb / 4 cups white fondant icing (see page 29)
cornflour (cornstarch), for dusting
assorted natural food colouring: black, grey, green, brown, yellow, pink
225 g / 8 oz / 1 cup prepared buttercream (see page 26)

Method

1. Level the tops of the cakes using a serrated knife, then brush the tops with apricot jam and stack together.

2. Take 250 g / 9 oz of the fondant and colour with dabs of green colouring. Roll out to 0.5 cm (¼ in) thickness on a work surface dusted with cornflour. Drape the fondant over the cake, smoothing down the top, sides and edges, then trim any excess.

3. Sit the cake on a cake board or stand. Beat the buttercream with a few drops of green colouring in a mixing bowl. Spoon into a piping bag fitted with a star-shaped nozzle and pipe blobs of the buttercream around the base of the cake.

4. Colour 200 g / 8 oz of the fondant with dabs of grey food colouring. Shape the grey fondant into an elephant's arms, legs, body and head. Use a damp paintbrush to help attach the limbs to the main body. Use a little white fondant to make tusks and eyes. Use a paring knife to add detail, then attach to the cake.

5. Take 150 g / 5 oz of the remaining fondant and colour with dabs of yellow colouring. Shape into a giraffe, preparing the legs and head separately. Build the giraffe and make two eyes with a little white fondant. Dilute some brown food colouring and dab onto the giraffe for spots. Attach to the cake.

6. Divide the remaining fondant into four. Colour one each black, brown and green, leaving the fourth white. Roll most of the black piece into the shape of a snake, then attach eyes and a tongue. Reserve the remaining black fondant.

7. Roll the brown piece into a thin log and divide into three, then attach to the cake like vines. Roll out the green fondant and cut out leaves to attach to the vines. Shape the remaining white fondant into a zebra's head. Use the remaining black fondant for detailing on the zebra's face. Dab some black food colouring onto the animals' eyes for pupils, to finish the cake.

Happy tiger cake

Serves: 12 Prep and cook time: 2 hours

Ingredients

For the cake:
2 x vanilla sponge cakes (see page 15)
110 g / 4 oz / ½ cup apricot jam (jelly), warmed

To decorate:
750 g / 1 lb 8 oz / 3 ⅓ cups white fondant icing (see page 29)
cornflour (cornstarch), for dusting
240 g / 8 oz / 1 cup apricot jam (jelly), warmed
150 g / 5 oz / ⅔ cup black fondant icing (see page 29)
assorted natural food colouring: red, pink, green, orange
orange ribbon

Method

1. Level the tops of the cakes using a serrated knife, then brush the top of one sponge with apricot jam. Position the other sponge on top.

2. Roll out 500 g / 1 lb 2 oz of the fondant to a 1 cm (½ in) thick round on a work surface dusted with cornflour. Brush the top of the cake with apricot jam, then drape the fondant over it, smoothing down for an even finish. Use a small cutter to give a fluted edge.

3. Roll out 150 g / 5 oz of the remaining white fondant to 2 cm (1 in) thickness. Using a stencil or freehand, cut out the shapes of two ears, a chin, the bridge of a nose and a top lip. Stick them to the cake using more jam as necessary.

4. Divide the remaining white fondant into three. Colour one each green, pink and red, kneading well. Shape the green into two eyes, the pink into a nose and the red into a tongue and attach to the cake using more jam.

5. Dilute the orange food colouring with a little water. Paint onto the cake where appropriate, including the nose. Leave to dry.

6. Roll out the black fondant to 2 cm (1 in) thickness. Cut out two eyebrows, six stripes, two pupils for the eyes and two thin strips. Attach the eyebrows and the pupils, the stripes on either side and the thin strips curling around the border of the ears. Tie the orange ribbon around the base of the cake to finish.

Under the sea cake

Serves: 10 Prep and cook time: 2 hours 45 minutes

Ingredients

For the cake:
2 x vanilla sponge cakes (see page 15)
75 g / 2 ½ oz / ⅓ cup apricot jam (jelly), warmed

To decorate:
750-850 g / 26-30 oz / 3 ½- 4 cups white fondant icing (see page 29)
110 g / 4 oz / ½ cup black fondant icing (see page 29)
cornflour (cornstarch), for dusting
assorted natural food colouring: orange, red, black, grey, purple, green
240-300 g / 8-11 oz / 1-1 ⅓ cups apricot jam (jelly)

Method

1. Level the tops of the cakes using a serrated knife, then brush the top of one sponge with apricot jam. Position the other sponge on top.

2. Divide the white fondant into six and roll into balls. Colour two balls with dabs of orange food colouring and knead until blended. Roll out one orange ball of fondant to about 1 cm (½ in) thickness on a work surface dusted with cornflour.

3. Brush the cake with jam. Drape the orange fondant over and smooth to an even finish, then trim the excess and reserve. Shape the other ball of orange fondant into a clown fish.

4. Dab two balls of white fondant with grey food colouring, then knead until uniform in colour and shape most of the fondant into a castle. Use more jam to help secure the castle to the top of the cake. Use a paring knife to add detail to the castle. Use the remaining grey fondant to make rocks and secure to the cake using more jam.

5. Shape one of the remaining balls of white fondant into a fish shape. Roll out the black fondant on a work surface dusted with cornflour to 0.5 cm (¼ in) thickness. Cut shapes from the icing to stick to the white fish, using the picture as a guide. Cut thin strips of black fondant and use any remaining white fondant to make the black and white stripes of the clown fish.

6. Colour the remaining fondant a variety of colours and shape into coral, starfish, shells and underwater vegetation. Attach to the cake using jam. Position the fish on top of the cake to finish.

Dinosaur cake

Serves: 12 Prep and cook time: 2 hours 30 minutes

Ingredients

For the cake:
1 x quantity vanilla sponge cake batter, unbaked (see page 15)

To decorate:
1 kg / 2 lb 2 oz / 4 ½ cups white fondant icing (see page 29)
cornflour (cornstarch), for dusting
150 g / 5 oz / ⅔ cup apricot jam (jelly), warmed
assorted natural food colouring: green, blue, grey, black, brown
225 g / 8 oz / 1 cup prepared buttercream (see page 26)

Method

1. Divide the cake batter between one lined 900 g / 2 lb pudding bowl and one lined 20 cm (8 in) cake tin. Bake until springy to touch and a cake tester comes out clean from the centres.

2. Remove to a wire rack to cool. Once cool, turn out and level the top of the rounded sponge using a serrated knife.

3. Roll out 100 g / 4 oz of the fondant to 0.5 cm (¼ in) thickness on a work surface dusted with cornflour. Cut out a 30 cm (12 in) round and attach to a cake board of the same size using a little jam to stick them together.

4. Spread a small round of buttercream onto the fondant and attach the flat side of the rounded sponge to it. Cut out the shape of a head, tail and four limbs from the second cake. Attach to the body of the dinosaur with more buttercream and coat the whole cake in a thin layer of buttercream.

5. Colour 700 g / 1 lb 5 oz of the fondant with green food colouring, kneading well. Roll out to 1 cm (½ in) thickness, then cut out pieces of fondant to cover the body, limbs, tail and head of the dinosaur. Smooth the fondant onto them, sealing well at the joins. Use the remaining green fondant to make spikes and attach them to the spine and head with a damp paintbrush.

6. Colour 175 g / 6 oz of the remaining fondant with grey colouring, kneading well. Divide and shape into rocks and stick them to the fondant on the cake board with a damp paintbrush.

7. Divide and shape the remaining 25 g / 1 oz of white fondant into two eyes. Attach to the head of dinosaur and add detail (using a paintbrush) with diluted blue and black colouring.

8. Use some diluted green colouring to colour the dinosaur, adding detail where appropriate. Use some diluted brown colouring to paint the fondant on the cake board. Add highlights and shadows to the rocks with some diluted grey colouring. Leave to dry.

Buzzy beehive cake

Serves: 12 Prep and cook time: 2 hours 30 minutes

Ingredients

For the cake:
1 x quantity vanilla sponge cake, unbaked (see page 15)

To decorate:
240 g / 8 oz / 1 cup apricot jam (jelly), warmed
600 g / 1 lb 3 oz / 2 ⅔ cups white fondant icing (see page 29)
cornstarch (cornflour), for dusting
few drops natural yellow food colouring
600 g / 1 lb 3 oz / 2 ½ cups prepared buttercream (see page 26)
few drops natural black food colouring
wire

Method

1. Spoon the batter into one lined 23 cm (9 in) cake tin and one lined 18 cm (7 in) tin. Bake until a cake tester comes out clean from their centres. Remove to a wire rack to cool. Once cool, turn out and level the tops using a serrated knife.

2. Spread the top of the 23 cm (9 in) cake with some apricot jam. Roll out 250 g / 9 oz of the fondant to 1 cm (½ in) thickness on a work surface dusted with cornflour. Drape over the cake, smoothing down the top and sides, then move the cake to a cake board.

3. Brush the 18 cm (7 in) cake with jam. Roll out 150 g / 5 oz of the remaining fondant to 1 cm (½ in) thickness. Drape over the cake, smoothing down the top and sides. Trim the excess at the base and attach the cake to the larger one using some jam. Reserve the excess white fondant.

4. Colour the buttercream with some yellow food colouring, then spoon into a piping bag fitted with a straight-sided nozzle. Pipe swirls of the buttercream around the top tier of the cake, building it up on top to a peak like a beehive, leaving space for a door on one side. Pipe a curve of buttercream around the door.

5. Colour the half the remaining fondant with some yellow colouring. Divide into balls and shape into bees. Add detail with black food colouring, such as stripes, eyes and mouths. Use any leftover yellow fondant to make the centre of the daisies.

6. Roll out the remaining fondant to 0.5 cm (¼ in) thickness and use a stencil cutter to cut out daisies. Cut wings for the bees with the excess and attach them to the bee bodies. Attach the yellow centres of the daisies to the white petals and arrange around the cake. To finish the cake, thread the bees onto pieces of wire and stick them to the cake.

creepy crawly spider cake

Serves: 12 Prep and cook time: 1 hour 20 minutes

Ingredients

For the cake:
2 x chocolate sponge cakes (see page 16)
110 g / 4 oz / ½ cup prepared buttercream (see page 26)

To decorate:
225 g / 8 oz / 1 cup prepared buttercream (see page 26)
green and black food colouring
50 g / 2 oz fondant icing (see page 29)
chocolate vermicelli
12 large red and yellow chocolate beans
white and black ready-to-use piping icing
8 liquorice sticks

Method

1. Level the tops of the cakes using a serrated knife, then brush the top of one sponge with the buttercream. Position the other sponge on top.

2. Colour 150 g / 5 oz / ½ cup of the buttercream with green food colouring, stirring until evenly coloured. Colour the remaining buttercream black, then set aside.

3. Spread the green buttercream over the cake using a palette knife, until the whole cake is evenly covered.

4. Roll the fondant icing into a ball, then coat in chocolate vermicelli until the fondant is no longer visible, to make the spider's body. Place the body in the centre of the cake. Draw eyes on two red chocolate beans using the ready-to-use icing and allow to dry. Attach the eyes to the body with a little piping icing.

5. Fill a piping bag with the reserved black buttercream and use a small-holed nozzle to pipe a spider's web on the cake.

6. Bend the liquorice sticks to make the legs, then and stick them into the spider's body and the cake.

7. To finish the cake, place the remaining chocolate beans around the cake to make miniature spiders. Use the black piping icing to give them legs and eyes.

Magic bunny cake

Serves: 12 Prep and cook time: 2 hours 45 minutes

Ingredients

For the cake:
2 x vanilla sponge cakes (see page 15)
110 g / 4 oz / ½ cup apricot jam (jelly), warmed

To decorate:
100 g / 4 oz brown fondant icing
240 g / 8 oz / 1 cup apricot jam (jelly)
100 g / 4 oz purple fondant icing
350 g / 11 oz white fondant icing
350 g / 11 oz black fondant icing (see page 29 for fondant recipe)
assorted natural food colouring: red, black, purple, brown, green
edible silver food paint
cake glitter

Method

1. Turn out the cakes from their tins and sandwich together with apricot jam. Roll out the brown fondant to 1 cm (½ in) thickness. Brush the top and sides of the cake with a thin layer of apricot jam, then drape the brown fondant over the cake, smoothing it over the sides and edges of the cake. Trim any excess.

2. Roll out the purple fondant to 1 cm (½ in) thickness, then cut into a round slightly larger than the top of the cake. Brush the top of the brown fondant with more apricot jam, then drape the purple fondant over it, smoothing it well on top. Stick parts of the purple fondant to the brown on the sides, to create texture.

3. Roll out 150 g / 5 oz of the white fondant and cut out eight card-shaped pieces using a paring knife. Stack four of them and decorate the top card using a paintbrush. Decorate the four remaining cards with different suits, then fan them out and use a little jam to stick them to the cake. Sit the deck of cards just over the corner of the fanned out cards.

4. Shape most of the black fondant into the magician's hat. Take a little white fondant and colour with dabs of red food colouring. Shape into a disk and a long strip and attach to the hat as shown in the picture.

5. Shape half of the remaining white fondant into a bunny. Use a little diluted red colouring and a clean paintbrush to colour as needed, then position the bunny on the hat. Divide the remaining fondant in three and colour the pieces red, green and black. Knead well until uniformly coloured. Shape the red into petals and the green into the stem of a rose. Position on top of the cake.

6. Roll the remaining black fondant into a wand. Attach to the top of the cake and decorate with edible silver food paint. Use a paring knife to score the fondant on the side of the cake with swirling patterns. Dust the cake with cake glitter to finish.

Tiered circus cake

Ingredients

For the cake:
1 ½ x quantity vanilla sponge cake batter, unbaked (see page 15)

To decorate:
1 kg / 2 lb 2 oz / 4 ½ cups white fondant icing (see page 29)
assorted natural food colouring: red, green, blue, orange, yellow, grey, brown, black
cornflour (cornstarch), for dusting
350 g / 12 oz / 1 ½ cups apricot jam (jelly)

Method

1. Divide the cake batter between two lined 23 cm (9 in) and two 18 cm (7 in) cake tins. Bake for 40–50 minutes until a cake tester comes out clean. Remove to a wire rack to cool. Once the cakes are cool, turn out from the tins. Brush all four cakes with apricot jam, then stack the 23 cm (9 in) cakes on top of each other. Do the same for the smaller cakes.

2. Roll out 250 g / 9 oz of the fondant icing and drape over the 23 cm (9 in) cakes, smoothing over the top, edges and sides. Brush the top and sides of the 18 cm (7 in) cake with more jam. Roll out 200 g / 7 oz of the fondant icing and drape over the cakes, smoothing over the top, edges and sides.

3. Brush the centre of the top of the 23 cm (9 in) cake with jam, then top with the smaller cake. Take four separate 100 g / 4 oz balls of fondant and colour each with dabs of blue, orange, yellow and green colouring respectively. Roll out each ball and cut some of it into strips of icing, as per the image, and secure to the bottom tier with more jam. Reserve the excess fondant.

4. With some of the reserved coloured fondant, cut flag shapes and thin strips of blue icing, then attach to the side of the top tier. Re-roll some of the remaining coloured fondant and shape into cubes. Divide the rest into three pieces and shape into squares. Attach these to the cubes and position on top of the cake.

5. Divide the remaining white fondant into three pieces and colour each grey, brown and dark yellow with food colouring. Using the image as a guide, shape the grey fondant into an elephant, the brown into a monkey and the yellow into the body of a lion.

6. Use some more brown and white fondant to create the mane for the lion and eyes for the animals. Use a piece of white fondant and colour it black. Create black pupils and attach the eyes of the animals, then position them on the cake to finish.

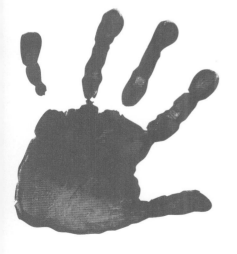

Piñata cake

Serves: 8 Prep and cook time: 1 hour 30 minutes

Ingredients

For the cake:
1 x quantity vanilla sponge cake
   batter, unbaked (see page 15)

To decorate:
400 g / 14 oz / 1 ¾ cups colourful
   chocolate sweets
2 tbsp sugar sprinkles

For the icing:
400 g / 14 oz / 1 ¾ cups prepared
   buttercream (see page 26)

Method

1. Preheat the oven to 180°C (160°C fan) / 350F / gas 4. Grease a 900 g / 2 lb pudding bowl with a little butter and grease and line the base of a 18 cm (7 in) cake tin with greaseproof paper.

2. Divide the batter between the prepared pudding bowl and cake tin. Bake for 45-55 minutes, removing the cake tin after 20-30 minutes, if golden and springy to the touch on top. A cake tester should come out clean when inserted in the centre.

3. Remove to a wire rack to cool. Once cool, use a serrated knife to hollow out the cake from the pudding bowl, leaving about 4 cm (1 ½ in) thickness of cake at the border. Fill with most of the chocolate sweets.

4. Turn out the cake from the cake tin and cut it to fit the top of the pudding bowl. Press the cake down on top using a little buttercream to stick the cakes together, then carefully invert the whole piñata cake onto a platter or stand.

5. Spread an initial layer of buttercream all over the piñata cake. Spread the rest evenly on top and decorate with sprinkles and the remaining sweets.

Ice cream cake

Serves: 12 Prep and cook time: 2 hours

Ingredients

For the cake:
1 x vanilla sponge cake (see page 15)

For the buttercream:
700 g / 1 lb 5 oz / 3 cups prepared buttercream (see page 26)
few drops natural blue food colouring

To decorate:
125 ml / 4 ½ fl. oz / ½ cup double (heavy) cream
2 tsp liquid glucose
250 g / 9 oz / 1 ⅔ cups dark chocolate, 70% solids, chopped
1 large ball fondant icing (see page 29)
1 ice cream cone
sugar stars and sprinkles

Method

1. Turn out the cake and level the top using a serrated knife.

2. In a bowl, add a few drops of blue food colouring to the buttercream and beat until uniformly coloured.

3. Spoon one-third of the icing into a piping bag fitted with a fluted nozzle. Use a spatula to cover the cake with a thin layer of the icing. Spread the rest of the icing over the top and sides of the cake. Lift the cake carefully onto a plate.

4. Pipe small blobs of buttercream around the base of the cake. Chill briefly.

5. Heat the cream and liquid glucose in a small saucepan until almost boiling. Place the chocolate in a heatproof bowl, then pour over the hot cream.

6. Leave to stand for 1 minute. Stir until smooth and leave to cool to 43°C / 110F. Place the ball of fondant onto the centre of the cake and attach the wafer to it. Pour over the cooled ganache, letting it run to the sides and set.

7. Decorate with stars and sprinkles to finish.

Rainbow cake

Serves: 12 Prep and cook time: 2 hours 15 minutes

Ingredients

For the cake:
1 x quantity vanilla sponge cake
   batter, unbaked (see page 15)

For the buttercream:
1 kg / 2 lb 2 oz / 4 ½ cups prepared
   buttercream (see page 26)
assorted natural food colouring:
   red, orange, yellow, green, blue,
   purple

To decorate:
50 g / 1 ¾ oz / 1 cup white
   marshmallows
10-12 chocolate coins

Method

1. Bake the cake in a lined 23 cm (9 in) round cake tin, until a cake tester comes out clean from the centre. Remove to a wire rack to cool.

2. Turn out from the tin and level the top using a serrated knife. Cut one-third of the cake away from one side to form the flat base of the rainbow, then reserve for use in other desserts. Use a smaller knife to cut out a semi-circle from the centre, leaving you with a rainbow shape.

3. Divide the buttercream between seven bowls. Add a few drops of each food colouring to six of the bowls respectively. Beat the colour into the buttercream until uniform.

4. Spoon the red buttercream into a piping bag fitted with a petal tip. Chill the other five coloured buttercreams. Cover the rainbow cake with a thin layer of white buttercream, then spread the remaining buttercream over the initial layer and smooth down.

5. Pipe two rows of folded petal shapes onto the top edge (and down the sides) of the cake, working the tip carefully up and down for each petal. Use the picture for guidance.

6. Spoon the other coloured buttercreams into piping bags fitted with petal tips.

7. Repeat step 5 for the other buttercream colours, working carefully and methodically. Once you get to the purple buttercream, pipe the first row as you did with the other colours, then fill in the inner side of the cake, working from the bottom upwards.

8. Place the marshmallows and chocolate coins at one end of the rainbow cake to finish.

Racing car cake

Serves: 12 Prep and cook time: 2 hours

Ingredients

For the cake:
1 x quantity vanilla sponge cake
   batter, unbaked (see page 15)

For the choux pastry:
55 g / 2 oz / ¼ cup unsalted butter
1 tbsp caster (superfine) sugar
170 ml / 6 fl. oz / ¾ cup water
75 g / 2 ½ oz / ½ cup plain
   (all-purpose) flour
2 medium eggs, beaten

To decorate:
900 g / 2 lb / 4 cups prepared
   buttercream (see page 26)
assorted natural food colouring:
   blue, green, pink, grey
white icing pen
large handful of jelly babies
2 tubes fruit polo sweets
chequered flags and start line
4 jelly cars

Method

1. Bake the cake in a 23 cm x 32 cm (9 in x 13 in) rectangular cake tin. Once cool, turn out and level the top using a serrated knife.

2. Combine the butter, sugar and water in a saucepan. Warm over a moderate heat until simmering, whisking frequently. Remove the pan from the heat and whisk in the flour, beating well until smooth and coming away from the sides of the pan. Beat in the egg in two additions until you have a smooth, shiny dough.

3. Spoon the pastry into a piping bag fitted with a straight-sided nozzle. Pipe the shape of a racetrack onto a non-stick baking tray. Increase the oven to 220°C (200°C fan) / 425F / gas 7.

4. Bake the pastry for 20–24 minutes until puffed and golden. Remove to a wire rack to cool.

5. Take 2 tbsp of the buttercream and add a few drops of pink colouring, beating well. Set aside. Divide the remaining buttercream between three bowls. Colour each respectively with green, blue and grey colouring. Beat well until uniformly coloured, then spoon the grey buttercream into a piping bag fitted with a straight-sided nozzle.

6. Cover the sides of the cake with the blue buttercream, spreading it evenly with a spatula. Top the cake with green buttercream, spreading it evenly.

7. Thickly pipe the grey buttercream on top of the pastry track. Use a white icing pen to decorate the buttercream with track marks. Sit the pastry on top of the green buttercream, then spoon the pink buttercream to the side of the track in the shape of a mound.

8. Decorate the cake with the jelly babies, fruit polos, flags and jelly cars.

Princess cake

Serves: 8 Prep and cook time: 1 hour 45 minutes

Ingredients

For the cake:
1 x quantity vanilla sponge cake
   batter, unbaked (see page 15)

For the buttercream:
750 g / 1 lb 6 oz / 3 ½ cups
   prepared buttercream (see
   page 26)
few drops natural pink food
   colouring

To decorate:
1 child's doll
6-8 fondant roses

Method

1. Preheat the oven to 170°C (150°C fan) / 325F / gas 3. Prepare the cake batter and spoon into a greased pudding bowl.

2. Bake for 40-50 minutes until a cake tester comes out clean from its centre. Remove to a wire rack to cool.

3. Once cool, use a wide spatula to help turn out the cake from the bowl. Level the top using a serrated knife and sit the flat side on a cake stand.

4. Gently beat together the buttercream with a few drops of food colouring until uniformly pink. Spoon most of the buttercream into a piping bag fitted with a small star-shaped nozzle.

5. Cover the cake with a thin layer of the remaining buttercream and chill for 15 minutes. Pipe roses of buttercream all over the sides of the cake, leaving the top undecorated for now.

6. Using a small thin skewer, bore two holes down through the top of the cake, approximately 4 cm (1 ½ in) width apart. Pass the legs of the doll down through the holes so that her body is sitting on top of the cake.

7. Continue to pipe around the base of the doll, then fashion her a dress with more buttercream roses. Decorate the princess' dress with sugarpaste roses to finish.

Knight's castle cake

Serves: 12 Prep and cook time: 2 hours 40 minutes

Ingredients

For the cake:
2 x quantity chocolate sponge cake batter, unbaked (see page 16)

For the chocolate buttercream:
350 g / 12 oz / 1 ½ cups prepared buttercream (see page 26)
350 g / 12 oz / 1 ½ cups prepared chocolate ganache (see page 30)

To decorate:
35–40 chocolate matchsticks
5 chocolate fingers
5 solid chocolate cones
1 tbsp liquid glucose
110 g / 4 oz / 1 cup chocolate sprinkles
30–34 chocolate-covered caramels
1 bourbon biscuit
1 chocolate button
1 chocolate toffee bar, halved
1 plastic knight

Method

1. Divide the cake batter between two greased and lined 20 cm (8 in) rectangular cake tins. Bake for 40–50 minutes until risen and springy to the touch. A cake tester should come out clean from their centres. Remove to a wire rack to cool.

2. Once cool, turn out. Split both cakes horizontally in half to give you four pieces of cake. Cut one of the pieces into four quarters.

3. Beat together the buttercream and the ganache until thoroughly combined. Using a spatula, cover the three large squares of cake with a thin layer of buttercream. Stack the squares on a platter or cake stand, then cover with more buttercream on the top and sides.

4. Coat three of the remaining quarters of cake with a thin layer of buttercream, then stack them on top of the base cake layer. Cover the sides and top with more buttercream. Sit the final quarter of cake upright on top of the cake and cover with buttercream.

5. Drag the tip of a butter knife up and down the buttercream to give it some texture. Attach chocolate matchsticks to the borders. Press the chocolate fingers against the front of the cake to look like a gate.

6. Brush the chocolate cones with a little liquid glucose, then roll in chocolate sprinkles. Position upright on the base cake, in the corners. Arrange the chocolate-covered caramels around the perimeter of the middle and top tiers.

7. Carefully separate the bourbon biscuit and cut each piece in half. Press into the cake to look like windows. Attach the chocolate button on the top tier, then position the chocolate toffee bars as a bridge to the cake. Stand the knight next to the cake to complete the knight's castle.

spring flowers cake

Serves: 12 Prep and cook time: 2 hours 30 minutes

Ingredients

For the cake:
1 x quantity fruit cake batter,
 unbaked (see page 19)

To decorate:
225 g / 8 oz / 1 cup caster
 (superfine) sugar
225 g / 8 oz / 2 cups ground
 almonds
2 medium eggs, beaten
1 tsp almond extract
assorted natural food colouring:
 red, yellow, blue
240 g / 8 oz / 1 cup white fondant
 icing (see page 29)
cornflour (cornstarch), for dusting

For the icing and garnish:
250 g / 9 oz / 2 cups icing
 (confectioners') sugar, sifted
few drops natural pink food
 colouring
pink icing pen
6 white chocolate chicks
1 tsp ground allspice

Method

1. Bake the fruit cake in a fluted 20 cm (8 in) cake tin. Once ready, remove to a wire rack to cool, then turn out of the tin.

2. Stir together the caster sugar and ground almonds in a mixing bowl. Beat in enough egg and the almond extract until you have a pliable dough. Turn out of the bowl and knead for 1 minute.

3. Break off a little of the almond paste and add a few dabs of red food colouring. Knead well until uniformly coloured, then divide into four and roll into small balls. Set aside. Take the rest of the almond paste and divide into 30 small balls.

4. Divide the fondant icing into three pieces. Colour each piece with dabs of red, yellow and blue food colouring respectively. Roll out each piece on a work surface dusted with cornflour to 0.5 cm (¼ in) thickness. Using a paring knife, cut out at least 20 petals of each colour, then thin the edges of the petals between your thumb and index finger. Set aside.

5. Place the icing sugar in a mixing bowl and whisk in a little boiling water, adding more as needed, until you have a smooth, pourable icing. Add a drop of the pink food colouring and mix well.

6. Cover the cake with the pink icing, spreading it over the sides and top. Arrange 25 of the almond paste balls in a small concentric circle in the centre of the cake. Draw the outline of petals on top of the cake with the icing pen, as per the image.

7. Arrange alternating balls of red and the remaining yellow almond paste balls around the perimeter of the cake, spaced apart. Carefully position fondant petals around them to create flowers. Make two additional red flowers, one more blue and one more yellow flower and set aside.

8. Sit a white chocolate chick on top of the almond paste balls. Present the cake with the additional fondant flowers and white chocolate chicks, as well as a dusting of ground allspice.

Aeroplane cake

Serves: 12 Prep and cook time: 2 hours 30 minutes

Ingredients

For the cake:
2 x vanilla sponge cakes (see page 15)
225 g / 8 oz / 1 cup prepared buttercream (see page 26)

To decorate:
1 kg / 2 lb 2 oz / 4 ½ cups white fondant icing (see page 29)
assorted natural food colouring: blue, red, orange, brown, black
cornflour (cornstarch), for dusting

Method

1. Levels the tops of the cakes using a serrated knife. Spread the top of one cake with buttercream and sandwich with the other cake. Spread the top and sides with a thin layer of buttercream.

2. Knead 300 g / 10 oz of the fondant with a little blue food colouring. Roll out to 1 cm (½ in) thickness on a work surface dusted with cornflour. Cut a large round to drape over the cake, smoothing it down over the top and sides.

3. Colour another 250 g / 9 oz of the fondant with red colouring. Shape 200 g / 7 oz into the body of the plane and roll out the rest to cut into the wings and tail. Attach to the body of the plane with a damp paintbrush to help them stick.

4. Take 250 g / 9 oz of white fondant and divide two-thirds of it into balls of various sizes to make clouds. Brush the undersides with a damp paintbrush and attach to the top of the cake, then sit the aeroplane with its wings resting on the clouds. Roll out the remaining third of fondant to 0.5 cm (¼ in) thickness, then cut out cloud shapes and attach them to the sides of the cake.

5. Colour 100 g / 4 oz of the remaining fondant orange. Shape most of it into the body of a man, rolling out the remainder to cut into strips and a propeller for the plane as well as any details for the body of the man. Attach the pieces according to the image.

6. Colour additional pieces of fondant brown, very light brown and black. Shape the brown fondant into hair, the light brown into arms and a head for the man, and the black to make detailing for the plane such as the centre of the propeller.

7. Attach the pieces using a damp paintbrush, then use any scraps of black and white fondant to make eyes and stick them to the man's head to finish the cake.

Giant cupcake cake

Serves: 12 Prep and cook time: 3 hours

Ingredients

For the cake:
2 x quantity vanilla sponge cake
   batter, unbaked (see page 15)
240 g / 8 oz / 1 cup apricot jam
   (jelly), warmed

To decorate:
1.2 kg / 2 lb 6 oz / 5 cups white
   fondant icing (see page 29)
assorted natural food colouring:
   blue, yellow, pink, red
cornflour (cornstarch), for dusting
500 g / 1 lb 2 oz / 2 ¼ cups royal
   icing (see page 28)
1 candy ruler, to garnish

Method

1. Divide the cake batter between two lined 18 cm (7 in), two lined 20 cm (8 in) and two lined 23 cm (9 in) cake tins. Bake until a cake tester comes out clean. Once cool, turn out and level the tops using a serrated knife. Brush the tops with apricot jam and stack the respective sponges on top of each other.

2. Colour 200 g / 7 oz of the fondant with blue colouring, then roll out and drape over the smallest cake, smoothing down. Use a pen to make indents on the side of the fondant. Trim any excess, re-roll and cut into long strips. Roll out 200 g / 7 oz of white fondant, drape over the 20 cm (8 in) cake and smooth down.

3. Colour 250 g / 9 oz of the fondant with a dab of pink colouring. Roll out the pink fondant to 0.75 cm (⅓ in) thickness. Drape over the 23 cm (9 in) cake, smoothing the top and sides. Sit the middle and top tiers on the base tier, with the smallest cake on top.

4. Mix the royal icing with a few drops of pink colouring, then spoon into a piping bag fitted with a wide slit nozzle and pipe rough swirls on top of the cake.

5. Divide the fondant into three and colour each yellow, pale pink and dark pink. Roll out to 0.5 cm (¼ in) and cut strips of varying widths. Reserve half of the yellow fondant and some of the pink. Attach the blue, yellow and pink strips to the side of the middle tier, using a damp paintbrush to help them stick.

6. Take most of the remaining yellow fondant and make a bow and ribbon. Cut assorted circles from the remaining coloured fondants, or shape into sweets and small balls. Attach them all over the tiered cake with a damp paintbrush.

7. Attach the bow and ribbon to the cake. Roll and shape any leftover fondant into cupcakes, using a paring knife to add detail. Position them on and around the cake and garnish with the candy ruler in the top.

Choo choo train cake

Serves: 12 Prep and cook time: 2 hours 30 minutes

Ingredients

For the cake:
1 x quantity vanilla sponge cake
batter, unbaked (see page 15)

For the buttercream:
750 g / 1 lb 6 oz / 3 ½ cups
prepared buttercream (see
page 26)
assorted natural food colouring:
red, yellow, blue

To decorate:
8 chocolate wafer fingers
10 double chocolate cookies
4 chocolate and vanilla sandwich
cookies
500 g / 18 oz / 2 cups wrapped
assorted chocolates
2 white chocolate sticks
small handful of marshmallows,
chopped
1 tsp liquid glucose
1 ice cream cone, painted blue with
diluted food colouring
1 almond wafer biscuit, cut into a
window shape
100 g / 3 ½ oz / 1 ½ cups
desiccated coconut
few drops of natural green food
colouring
plastic animals

Method

1. Spoon the cake batter into a greased and lined 23 cm x 33 cm
(9 in x 13 in) rectangular cake tin. Bake for 45-55 minutes until
a cake tester comes out clean. Remove to a wire rack to cool.

2. Take half of the buttercream and divide it between two bowls,
adding a few drops of yellow and red food colouring respectively
to each bowl. Beat each until uniformly coloured. Add drops of blue
colouring to the remaining buttercream and beat well.

3. Turn out the cake and cut into quarters. Use a serrated knife
to trim three of the pieces into rectangular carriages. Carefully
trim the final quarter into a cylinder shape. Use a little of the blue
buttercream to attach the cylinder to one of the carriages,
then cover the whole engine in a thin layer of blue buttercream.

4. Position the blue engine on a platter and cover with more
buttercream. Using the same method, cover the remaining
carriages with the yellow and red buttercream respectively.
Position them behind the front of the train.

5. Arrange the chocolate wafer fingers next to the base of the train
to create tracks. Attach the different cookies as wheels, using a
little buttercream to help them stick. Cut a rectangular hole out of
the top of the yellow carriage and fill with chocolates. Bore two
small holes at the back of the red carriage using a skewer and
position the white chocolate sticks upright in them.

6. Dip edges of the marshmallows in liquid glucose to attach them
to other pieces of marshmallow. Once you have a cluster, brush
the bottom with more liquid glucose and attach it to the top of
the ice cream cone. Bore a hole in the top of the blue carriage and
position the cone in it.

7. Attach the almond wafer biscuit to the side of the blue carriage.
Pulse together the desiccated coconut and a drop of green
colouring in a food processor. Scatter the grass next to the
train and present with the plastic animals.

sports cake

Serves: 12 Prep and cook time: 2 hours

Ingredients

For the cake:
1 x quantity vanilla sponge cake
  batter, unbaked (see page 15)

To decorate:
110 g / 4 oz / ½ cup prepared
  buttercream (see page 26)
600 g / 1 lb 3 oz / 2 ⅔ cups white
  fondant icing (see page 29)
few drops natural brown food
  colouring
cornflour (cornstarch), for dusting
240 g / 8 oz / 1 cup apricot jam
  (jelly), warmed

Method

1. Divide the cake batter between two oval-shaped cake tins.
   Bake until a cake tester comes out clean, then remove to a
   wire rack to cool.

2. Once cool, turn out and level the tops of the cakes if peaked.
   Use a serrated knife to shape the cakes into rugby ball halves.

3. Spread the flat top of one of the cakes with buttercream, then
   sandwich against the other to give you the shape of the ball.

4. Colour 500 g / 1 lb 2 oz of the fondant with brown colouring,
   kneading until uniformly coloured and pliable. Roll out to 0.75 cm
   (⅓ in) thickness on a work surface dusted with cornflour, then cut
   out four oval-shaped panels, each to cover a quarter of the cake.

5. Brush the cake with apricot jam. Carefully attach the fondant
   panels to the side of the cake until completely covered, then
   smooth down.

6. Roll the remaining white fondant to 0.5 cm (¼ in) thickness
   and cut out two rings approximately 3 cm (1 ½ in) in width.
   Brush the rings with water using a paintbrush, then attach
   the damp side to the ends of the cake, as per the image.

7. Cut a seam from the remaining white fondant as well as markers.
   Attach to the centre seam of the football, then use a cocktail stick
   to make stitching details between the seams of the fondant to
   complete the cake.

cupcake tower

Ingredients

For the cake:
1 x quantity vanilla sponge cake batter, unbaked (see page 15)

For the cupcakes:
225 g / 8 oz / 1 cup butter, softened
225 g / 8 oz / 1 cup caster (superfine) sugar
4 eggs, beaten
225 g / 8 oz / 2 cups self-raising flour
1 tsp vanilla extract

For the icing:
400 g / 14 oz / 4 cups icing (confectioners') sugar
2 tsp vanilla extract
3-4 tbsp hot water
assorted natural food colouring: yellow, blue, lilac, green, pink

To decorate:
coloured sugar sweets
long candles

Method

1. Bake the cake batter in a greased and lined 23 cm (9 in) cake tin until golden and springy to the touch. Remove to a wire rack to cool, then turn out of the tin.

2. Reduce the oven temperature to 180°C (160°C fan) / 350F / gas 4 and line a 12-hole muffin tin and a 12-hole mini muffin tin with paper cases.

3. Beat the butter and sugar until light and creamy, then gradually beat in the eggs until well blended. Sift in the flour and fold in gently with the vanilla, until just combined.

4. Spoon into the paper cases and bake the mini cupcakes for 10-15 minutes and the larger cupcakes for 20-25 minutes until golden and springy to the touch. Cool for 5 minutes in the tin, then place on a wire rack to cool completely.

5. Sift the icing sugar into a bowl and gradually stir in the vanilla and water until smooth and thick. Divide the mixture into five smaller bowls and add a few drops of colouring to each bowl.

6. Spread different colours of icing onto the cakes, covering the sides and top of the larger cake. Attach the sweets to the base of the large cake and on top of the cupcakes, then decorate with candles. Place the smaller cakes on the large cake and leave to set.

Pirate ship cake

Serves: 12 Prep and cook time: 3 hours

Ingredients

For the cake:
2 x quantity vanilla sponge cake
    batter, unbaked (see page 15)
240 g / 8 oz / 1 cup apricot jam
    (jelly), warmed

To decorate:
200 g / 7 oz blue fondant icing
400 g / 14 oz brown fondant icing
200 g / 7 oz yellow fondant icing
100 g / 4 oz red fondant icing
50 g / 2 oz grey fondant icing
50 g / 2 oz green fondant icing
50 g / 2 oz red fondant icing
    (see page 29 for fondant icing
    recipe)
assorted natural food colouring:
    black, brown, blue, white
2 lollipop sticks
3 brown drink stirrers
white card

Method

1. Divide the batter between four greased and lined oval cake tins and bake until a cake tester comes out clean from their centres. Level the tops using a serrated knife. Brush the tops of three with jam and stack the four cakes on top of each other. Using the image as a guide, cut away parts of the cake to make steps.

2. Roll out the blue fondant, then cut out a 30 cm (12 in) round and secure to a cake board of the same size. Roll out the brown fondant and cut two large strips, then brush the sides of the lower half of the cake with jam and secure the fondant to them.

3. Attach the remaining brown fondant to the top of the cake to cover the steps. Gather the excess and make 16 wooden spindles as well as five planks. Position the spindles and planks at both ends of the ship's deck, using the picture as a guide.

4. Roll out the yellow fondant and cut out four rectangles for the front of the cake (two rectangles should be twice the height of the other two). Secure to the top sides of the cake using a little jam. Cut out one large step pattern piece to wrap around the back of the cake and secure to the cake with more jam.

5. Roll out the red fondant and cut thin strips to border the yellow fondant. Cut out 10 circles of thin red fondant and secure to the side of the ship to make portholes.

6. Roll out the grey fondant and cut out an anchor, then secure to the front of the cake. Shape the green fondant into a parrot, using any excess coloured fondant for detail. Paint on black pupils. Shape the pink fondant into a pirate's head, detailing with leftover fondant. Stick on lollipop sticks and into the cake.

7. To finish, dilute some brown colouring and paint onto the ship to create plank details. Use blue and white colouring for the sea, pinching the fondant to create texture. Make sails with card and thread onto the drink stirrers, then position as masts. Use more black colouring to paint on portholes, and a skull and crossbones.

Volcano cake

Serves: 8 Prep and cook time: 1 hour 30 minutes

Ingredients

For the cake:
1 x quantity chocolate sponge cake
  batter, unbaked (see page 16)

For the icing:
375 g / 13 oz / 3 cups icing
  (confectioners') sugar, sifted
assorted natural food colouring:
  orange, pink

To decorate:
3 chocolate honeycomb bars,
  chopped
100 g / 3 ½ oz / ½ cup sugar-
  coated chocolate sweets
55 g / 2 oz / ¼ cup mini sugar-
  coated chocolate sweets
150 g / 5 oz / 1 cup jelly beans
8 lollipops
orange cellophane flames

Method

1. Preheat the oven to 170°C (150°C fan) / 325F / gas 3 and spoon the cake batter into a bundt tin. Bake for 50-60 minutes or until a cake tester inserted in the centre comes out clean, then remove to a wire rack to cool. Once the cake is cool, turn out and invert onto a serving plate.

2. Divide the icing sugar between two bowls and add a little boiling water to each, whisking until smooth and pourable. Colour one orange and one pink, whisking well until uniformly coloured.

3. Arrange the chocolate honeycomb around the base of the cake. Pour the pink icing over the cake, letting it run down the sides. Pour the orange over the pink icing to mix them.

4. Decorate the cake with the sugar-coated chocolates and some jelly beans. Stud the top with lollipops and thread some jelly beans onto thin wire to stick in the top of the cake. Finish with orange cellophane flames.

Cupcakes and
cake pops

Football cupcakes

Serves: 12 Prep and cook time: 1 hour

Ingredients

For the cupcakes:
12 vanilla cupcakes (see page 24)

To decorate:
110 g / 4 oz / ½ cup prepared
  buttercream (see page 26)
600 g / 1 lb 3 oz / 2 ½ cups white
  fondant icing (see page 29)
few drops natural green food
  colouring
48 foil-covered mini chocolate
  footballs

Method

1. Level the tops of the cupcakes using a serrated knife, then spread with a thin layer of the buttercream.

2. Knead the fondant with a few drops of green colouring until uniform in colour and very pliable.

3. Divide the fondant into 12 pieces and press each piece through a sieve, then cut away the grass with a sharp knife.

4. Lift the grass onto the buttercream and press down gently. Garnish with the chocolate footballs on top.

Treasure island cupcakes

Serves: 12 Prep and cook time: 1 hour 30 minutes

Ingredients

For the cupcakes:
12 vanilla cupcakes (see page 24)

To decorate:
240 g / 8 oz / 1 cup apricot jam
   (jelly), warmed
1 kg / 2 lb 2 oz / 4 ½ cups white
   fondant icing (see page 29)
cornflour (cornstarch), for dusting
assorted natural food colouring:
   red, pink, black, grey, gold/
   yellow, blue, green

Method

1. Level the tops of the cupcakes using a serrated knife.

2. Colour 200 g / 7 oz of the fondant icing with black food colouring and knead until uniformly coloured. Roll out on a work surface dusted with cornflour, then cut out four rounds the same size as the cupcakes.

3. Brush the tops of four cupcakes with jam and secure the black fondant rounds to them. Reserve the excess.

4. Colour another 200 g / 7 oz of the fondant with pink colouring. Roll out and cut out four rounds the same size as the cupcakes. Brush the top of four cupcakes with jam and secure the pink fondant rounds to them. Reserve the excess.

5. Colour 100 g / 4 oz of white fondant with blue colouring, then roll out and cut out two rounds the same size as the cupcakes. Brush the top of two cupcakes with jam and secure the blue rounds to them. Reserve the excess and roll out to 0.5 cm (¼ in) thickness.

6. Repeat step 5 with white icing, securing them to the top of two cupcakes. Reserve the excess white fondant and re-roll to 0.5 cm (¼ in) thickness.

7. Divide the remaining fondant into four pieces and colour each grey, red, gold and green. Knead each piece until uniformly coloured. Use the coloured fondants to make shapes to decorate your cupcakes, such as an anchor, pirates, a parrot, flags and gold coins.

8. Use a damp paintbrush to secure the fondant shapes to the cupcakes. To finish the cake, dilute a little black colouring and use to paint skull and crossbones onto the flags and to add coloured detailing to the parrots.

Riding school cupcakes

Serves: 12 Prep and cook time: 2 hours

Ingredients

For the cupcakes:
12 vanilla cupcakes (see page 24)

For the buttercream:
225 g / 8 oz / 1 cup prepared
    buttercream (see page 26)
few drops natural blue food
    colouring

To decorate:
750 g / 1 lb 6 oz / 3 ½ cups white
    fondant icing (see page 29)
cornflour (cornstarch), for dusting
assorted natural food colouring:
    blue, red, grey, black
110 g / 4 oz / ½ cup apricot jam
    (jelly), warmed
fondant daisies
white icing pen

Method

1. Level the tops of the cupcakes using a serrated knife.

2. Add a drop of blue food colouring to the buttercream and beat well until uniformly light blue, adding more colouring as needed. Spread the buttercream on top of the cupcakes, smoothing to a flat finish.

3. Knead 350 g / 12 oz of fondant with a few drops of blue food colouring until light blue and uniform in colour. Roll out to 1 cm (½ in) thickness on a work surface dusted with cornflour, then use a fluted cutter to cut 12 rounds the same size as the cakes.

4. Use a pen to make grooves in the fondant, then press down the rounds gently on top of the buttercream.

5. Add a few dabs of red food colouring to 200 g / 7 oz of the remaining fondant. Knead until uniformly coloured. Set aside a small ball of red fondant, then shape the rest into riding hats and attach to some of the cupcakes using jam.

6. Divide the remaining white fondant into three and colour one piece with a few dabs of grey food colouring, kneading until uniform in colour. Shape into horse heads and attach to some of the cupcakes with jam. Colour another piece with a speck of black colouring, kneading until uniform. Make eyes and hair for the horses with the black fondant, attaching with jam.

7. Roll out the remaining white fondant to 0.5 cm (¼ in) thickness on a work surface dusted with cornflour. Cut out small triangles and attach them to the riding hats with a dab of jam. Roll out the reserved red fondant and cut thin strips to attach to the horses as bridles. Decorate with fondant daises and dots of white icing, using the icing pen.

95

Stripy cupcakes

Serves: 12 Prep and cook time: 1 hour 35 minutes

Ingredients

For the cupcakes:
1 x quantity vanilla cupcake batter, unbaked (see page 24)
2 unwaxed lemons, zest finely grated

To decorate:
400-500 g / 14-18 oz white fondant icing (see page 29)
assorted natural food colouring: pink, lilac, orange, blue, yellow, green, red
cornflour (cornstarch), for dusting
icing (confectioners') sugar, for dusting

For the icing:
200 g / 7 oz / 2 cups icing (confectioners') sugar
hot water
few drops vanilla extract

Method

1. Make the cupcake batter as directed on page 24, adding the lemon zest with the flour. Bake until a cake tester comes out clean, then remove to a wire rack to cool.

2. Once cool, level the tops of the cupcakes using a serrated knife.

3. Divide the fondant icing into seven equal portions and knead a few drops of food colouring into each portion, so you have seven different colours.

4. With your hands, roll each portion into a long, thin rope and brush the edges of each rope with a little water.

5. Lay the ropes side by side on a surface dusted with cornflour and icing sugar and press the edges together so that they stick.

6. Roll very lightly with a rolling pin over the top to flatten slightly. Cut out 12 rounds with a cutter, the same diameter as the cakes.

7. Sift the icing sugar into a bowl and beat in enough hot water and the vanilla to make a thin, smooth icing. Spread the icing on the cakes.

8. Press the striped rounds on each cake before the icing sets and leave to set.

Starry cupcakes

Serves: 12 Prep and cook time: 1 hour 15 minutes

Ingredients

For the cupcakes:
12 vanilla cupcakes (see page 24)

For the buttercream:
450 g / 16 oz / 2 cups prepared
   buttercream (see page 26)

To decorate:
450 g / 16 oz / 2 cups white
   fondant icing (see page 29)
assorted natural food colouring:
   red and blue
cornflour (cornstarch), for dusting
edible glitter
assorted sprinkles
sugared almonds (optional)

Method

1. Level the tops of the cupcakes using a serrated knife.

2. Spoon the buttercream into a piping bag fitted with a wide star-shaped nozzle. Pipe swirls of buttercream on top of the cupcakes, working to a peak in the centre.

3. Divide the fondant in two and colour one piece red and one blue, kneading well until uniform in colour. Roll out the fondant icing to 1 cm (½ in) thickness on a work surface dusted with cornflour. Use a small star-shaped cutter to cut out 12 stars from each colour of fondant.

4. Position the fondant stars on the buttercream. Dust with edible glitter and decorate with sprinkles.

Night owl cupcakes

Serves: 12 Prep and cook time: 1 hour 30 minutes

Ingredients

For the cupcakes:
12 vanilla cupcakes (see page 24)

To decorate:
450 g / 16 oz / 2 cups prepared
    buttercream (see page 26)
550 g / 1 lb 2 oz / 2 ½ cups white
    fondant icing (see page 29)
assorted natural food colouring:
    green, yellow, black
cornflour (cornstarch), for dusting

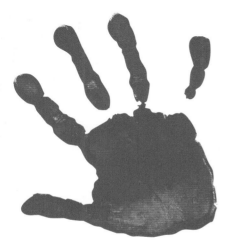

Method

1. Level the tops of the cupcakes using a serrated knife.

2. Spoon the buttercream into a piping bag fitted with a wide star-shaped nozzle. Pipe swirls of buttercream onto the cupcakes, working to a peak in the centre.

3. Break off a small ball of fondant and set aside. Divide the remaining fondant into two pieces and colour one with a few dabs of the green colouring and the other with a speck or two of yellow colouring. Knead until uniformly coloured. Roll out both colours of fondant on a work surface dusted with cornflour to 0.5 cm (¼ in) thickness.

4. Using a stencil or working freehand, cut out six owl bodies from each colour of fondant. With the rest of the fondant, cut out 12 wings and feet from each colour, then six noses from each colour.

5. Use a damp paintbrush to help stick the wings, feet and noses to the bodies of the owls. Roll out the reserved ball of white fondant to 0.5 cm (¼ in) thickness. Use a small cutter to punch out 24 eyes for the owls. Attach them to the owls above their noses. Take any scraps of fondant and roll into tiny pupils, attaching them to the eyes.

6. Brush on the pupils with black food colouring. If desired, use a thin, sharp paring knife or icing embosser to make feather patterns in the bodies of the owls. Attach the owls to the cupcakes to finish.

Zebra cupcakes

Serves: 12 Prep and cook time: 2 hours

Ingredients

For the cupcakes:
12 vanilla cupcakes (see page 24)

To decorate:
1.5 kg / 3 lb 3 oz / 6 ⅔ cups white
　fondant icing (see page 29)
assorted natural food colouring:
　green, black, pink
110 g / 4 oz / ½ cup apricot jam
　(jelly), warmed
cornflour (cornstarch)

Method

1. Level the tops of the cupcakes using a serrated knife.

2. Take 900 g / 2 lb of the white fondant and divide into 12 even pieces. Divide each piece into smaller balls and shape into arms, legs, a body and head for the zebras. Secure the legs, arms and head to the bodies with a damp paintbrush. Set aside.

3. Add a dab of green food colouring to 250 g / 9 oz of the remaining white fondant and knead well. Divide the fondant into 12 and knead into rounds. Press the rounds of fondant through a fine sieve, cutting away with a paring knife to create grass.

4. Brush the tops of the cupcakes with warmed jam, then secure the grass fondant to them. Break off 100 g / 4 oz of fondant from the remaining amount and roll out to 0.5 cm (¼ in) thickness on a work surface dusted with cornflour.

5. Cut into ovals for the zebra noses, then brush with a damp paintbrush and secure to the zebra heads. Dilute some black food colouring with water and paint the noses grey, then make indents for nostrils and a mouth.

6. Pinch off a small amount of white fondant and colour pink with a little food colouring. Roll out and shape into ears, then attach to the zebra heads. Paint the insides dark pink with a little more food colouring.

7. Colour the remaining fondant with dabs of black colouring. Knead well and roll out on a work surface dusted with cornflour. Cut out 12 rounds slightly smaller than the top of the cupcakes, then position them on top of the grass.

8. Sit the zebras carefully on top of the fondant, using a little jam to help adhere. With the remaining black fondant, cut out hooves, stripes and manes, then use a damp paintbrush to help stick the pieces to the zebras. Use a little more black colouring to paint on the zebras' eyes to finish.

Frog cupcakes

Serves: 12 Prep and cook time: 1 hour 40 minutes

Ingredients

For the cupcakes:
12 vanilla cupcakes (see page 24)

To decorate:
500 g / 18 oz / 2 ¼ cups white
    fondant icing (see page 29)
few drops natural blue food
    colouring
2 tbsp vegetable shortening, chilled
    in the freezer and then grated
cornflour (cornstarch), for dusting
110 g / 4 oz / ½ cup prepared
    buttercream (see page 26)
few drops natural green food
    colouring

Method

1. Level the tops of the cupcakes using a serrated knife.

2. Take 200 g / 7 oz of the fondant and colour with a few dabs
   of blue food colouring. Add the grated shortening and knead
   well until uniformly blue, then roll out on a work surface dusted
   with a little cornflour.

3. Cut out rounds of the fondant the same size as the cupcakes.
   Spread the tops of the cupcakes with a little buttercream, then top
   with the fondant rounds.

4. Break off 100 g / 4 oz of the remaining fondant and divide in
   two. Divide one piece into 24 and roll into balls to make the eyes.
   Set aside. Add a few specks of green colouring to the other
   piece and knead until uniformly light green in colour.

5. Roll out on a work surface dusted with cornflour. Using a small
   stencil or cutter, cut out 24 flowers. Set aside.

6. Colour the remaining piece of fondant with a few dabs of green
   food colouring. Knead until uniformly coloured. Break off 12 balls to
   make the frog bodies and roll between your palms. Attach to the
   blue fondant on the cupcakes.

7. With the remaining green fondant, break into pea-sized pieces
   and roll into balls. Position around the frog bodies to make legs
   and arms. Attach the prepared eyes and flowers. Use a small
   paring knife to make mouths and holes in the eyes.

8. Use the tip of the paring knife to carefully lift some of the
   blue fondant to give the appearance of bubbles.

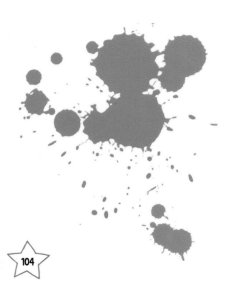

Caterpillar cupcakes

Serves: 12 Prep and cook time: 1 hour 30 minutes

Ingredients

For the cupcakes:
12 vanilla cupcakes (see page 24)

For the buttercream:
450 g / 16 oz / 2 cups prepared
    buttercream (see page 26)
few drops natural green food
    colouring

To decorate:
12 jelly sweets
assorted fizzy lances
½ strawberry lance
2 fruit ring sweets
2 mini chocolate sweets
2 lollipops

Method

1. Level the tops of the cupcakes using a serrated knife.

2. Beat the buttercream with a few drops of green colouring until uniformly light green. Spoon into a piping bag fitted with a wide star-shaped nozzle. Pipe the buttercream in swirls on top of the cupcakes.

3. Place a jelly sweet on top of each cupcake. Cut the fizzy lances in half and press into the sides of the cupcakes to make legs for the caterpillar.

4. Place the jelly sweet cupcakes in a wiggling line to make the body of the caterpillar.

5. Decorate the final cupcake with a strawberry lance for a mouth, the fruit ring sweets as eyes and the mini chocolate sweets for pupils. Stick the lollipops into the top to make antenna.

6. Stick the cupcake sideways onto the front cupcake to finish the caterpillar.

Candy cupcakes

Serves: 12 Prep and cook time: 50 minutes

Ingredients

For the cupcakes:
12 vanilla cupcakes (see page 24)

To decorate:
450 g / 16 oz / 2 cups prepared
    buttercream (see page 26)
few drops natural green food
    colouring
200 g / 7 oz / 1 cup dolly mixture
    sweets
12 lollipops
120 g / 4 oz / 1 cup sugar sprinkles

Method

1. Level the tops of the cupcakes using a serrated knife.

2. Mix together the buttercream and a few drops of green food colouring until evenly coloured. Spoon into a piping bag fitted with a star-shaped nozzle.

3. Pipe swirls on top of the cupcakes, keeping the buttercream in one layer. Decorate with dolly mixture sweets, lollipops and sugar sprinkles.

Birthday present pops

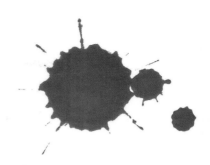

Serves: 24 Prep and cook time: 2 hours

Ingredients

For the cake pops:
½ x vanilla sponge cake (see page 15)
225 g / 8 oz / 1 cup prepared buttercream (see page 26)

To decorate:
500 g / 18 oz / 2 ¼ cups white fondant icing (see page 29)
few drops natural blue food colouring
cornflour (cornstarch)
240 g / 8 oz / 1 cup apricot jam (jelly), warmed
225 g / 8 oz / 1 cup caster (superfine) sugar
75 g / 2 ½ oz / ⅓ cup liquid glucose
55 ml / 2 fl. oz / ¼ cup water
few drops natural red food colouring
24 mini blue sweets
24 lollipop sticks
240 g / 8 oz / 2 cups sugar sprinkles

Method

1. Crumble the sponge cake into a food processor and pulse until you have cake crumbs.

2. Tip into a mixing bowl and combine with the buttercream, mixing evenly until you have a cake dough. Divide the mixture and shape into 24 box shapes.

3. Add a few dabs of blue food colouring to the fondant and knead well until uniform in colour. Roll out to 0.75 cm (⅓ in) thickness on a work surface dusted with cornflour and cut out 24 squares to cover the pops.

4. Brush the pops with apricot jam, then stick the fondant to them, smoothing well all over and sealing well on one side. Set aside on a tray.

5. Combine the sugar, liquid glucose and water in a saucepan, stirring briefly. Heat until the syrup registers 140°C / 284F on a sugar thermometer. Remove from the heat, add a few drops of red food colouring and swirl until uniformly coloured. Leave to cool briefly.

6. Carefully spoon the red caramel over the pops in the shape of ribbon and bow. Stick a mini blue sweet on top of the bows.

7. Slide the cake pops onto lollipop sticks and sit the pops upright in cups of sprinkles to serve.

Assorted cake pops

Serves: 24 Prep and cook time: 1 hour 15 minutes

Ingredients

For the pops:
1 x vanilla sponge cake (see page 15)
225 g / 8 oz / 1 cup prepared buttercream (see page 26)
24 lollipop sticks

To decorate:
450 g / 16 oz / 3 cups white chocolate, chopped
225 ml / 8 fl. oz / 1 cup double (heavy) cream
assorted natural food colouring: green, pink, yellow, purple
assorted coloured sugar sprinkles
100 g / 3 ½ oz / ⅔ cup dark chocolate, chopped

Method

1. Crumble the sponge cake into a food processor and pulse until you have cake crumbs.

2. Tip into a mixing bowl and add the prepared buttercream, mixing well until a cake dough forms. Shape into 24 pops and set aside. Skewer with the lollipop sticks and stand upright in a polystyrene box, then chill for 30 minutes.

3. Place the white chocolate in a heatproof bowl and warm the cream in a saucepan until almost boiling. Pour the hot cream over the chocolate and leave for 1 minute.

4. Stir until melted and even. Divide between five bowls and colour four with a little green, pink, yellow and purple colouring respectively. Dip the pops into the melted chocolate, turning to coat. Sit upright in a polystyrene box and sprinkle the coloured pops with sugar sprinkles.

5. Melt the dark chocolate in a bain-marie set over a half-filled saucepan of simmering water, stirring frequently. Once melted, drizzle over the white chocolate pops as well as some of the other coloured ones. Chill for 30 minutes before serving.

White chocolate pops

Serves: 24 Prep and cook time: 1 hour 15 minutes

Ingredients

For the pops:
1 x chocolate sponge cake (see page 16)
175 g / 6 oz / ¾ cup prepared chocolate ganache (see page 30)
55 g / 2 oz / ¼ cup unsalted butter, softened

To decorate:
24 assorted party sticks or skewers
300 g / 11 oz / 2 cups white chocolate, chopped
120 g / 4 oz / 1 cup sugar sprinkles

Method

1. Crumble the sponge cake into a food processor and pulse until you have cake crumbs.

2. Tip into a mixing bowl and add the chocolate ganache and butter, mixing well until a cake dough forms. Shape into 24 pops and set aside. Skewer with the party sticks and set upright in a polystyrene box. Chill for 30 minutes.

3. Place the chocolate in a heatproof bowl and microwave in 15-second bursts until melted, stirring in between.

4. Once melted, dip the pops into the melted chocolate, turning to coat. Sit upright in a polystyrene box and sprinkle their tops with sugar sprinkles. Chill for 30 minutes before serving.

Chocolate sprinkle pops

Serves: 18 Prep and cook time: 1 hour 15 minutes

Ingredients

For the pops:
½ x vanilla sponge cake
  (see page 15)
225 g / 8 oz / 1 cup prepared
  buttercream (see page 26)

To decorate:
18 lollipop sticks
300 g / 11 oz / 2 cups dark
  chocolate, chopped
100 ml / 3 ½ fl. oz / ½ cup double
  (heavy) cream
120 g / 4 oz / 1 cup sugar sprinkles

Method

1. Crumble the sponge cake into a food processor and pulse until you have cake crumbs.

2. Tip into a mixing bowl and add the prepared buttercream, mixing well until a cake dough forms. Shape into 18 pops and set aside. Skewer with the lollipop sticks and set upright in a polystyrene box. Chill for 30 minutes.

3. Place the chocolate in a heatproof bowl and warm the cream in a saucepan until almost boiling. Pour the hot cream over the chocolate and leave for 1 minute.

4. Stir until melted and even. Dip the pops into the melted chocolate, turning to coat. Sit upright in a polystyrene box and sprinkle with sugar sprinkles. Chill for 30 minutes before serving.

Owl cake pops

Serves: 18 Prep and cook time: 1 hour

Ingredients

For the pops:
½ x vanilla sponge cake recipe (see page 15)
225 g / 8 oz / 1 cup prepared buttercream (see page 26)

To decorate:
200 g / 7 oz / 1 ⅓ cups dark chocolate, chopped
200 g / 7 oz / 1 ⅓ cups milk chocolate, chopped
200 ml / 7 fl. oz / ¾ cup double (heavy) cream
18 skewers
36 chocolate sweets
36 pistachios, shelled
36 mini ring sweets
18 mini chocolate sweets
36 small sugar stars

Method

1. Crumble the sponge cake into a food processor and pulse until you have cake crumbs.

2. Tip into a bowl and add the buttercream, mixing well until it forms a cake dough. Divide and shape into 18 egg shapes.

3. Place the dark chocolate in a heatproof bowl and warm the cream until boiling in a saucepan. Pour the hot cream over the chocolate, leave for 1 minute, then stir until smooth.

4. Dip the end of the skewers in the ganache. Skewer through the centre of the cake pops, then sit the skewers upright in a polystyrene box. Chill for 20 minutes.

5. Gently warm the milk chocolate in a microwave, heating in 10-second bursts, until pourable. Dip the chilled pops in the chocolate, turning to coat. Sit upright in the polystyrene box and chill for 10 minutes.

6. As the chocolate sets, attach the chocolate sweets as wings, pistachios as ears, mini ring sweets as eyes, mini chocolate sweets as noses and sugar stars as feet, to make the owls. Chill for another 45 minutes until set.

It's party time!

Now that you have the perfect cake, why not show it off? If you're having a party or a family get-together, here are some ideas to make it even more special for your kids.

Invitations

If you're feeling crafty, why not make your own invitations? This is a great activity for you to do with your kids, especially if you have any craft supplies around the house, such as card, craft paper, pipe cleaners, sequins, stickers or glitter.

A really fun, interactive way to send party invites is by balloon! Simply inflate your balloons, write the details on the side, then deflate the balloons before handing them out.

Use the template below to make sure you give out all the details:

Name...
You are invited to ....'s party!
Date...
Time...
Venue...
Theme...
RSVP...

Venue

The cheapest way to throw a party is at home, but that isn't always an option if you don't have space. If you do decide to host, it's a good idea to move all your breakables out of the way (vases and ornaments are prime candidates) in case of an excitable accident. Clear a big space inside or open the doors to your back garden, to give the kids plenty of space to spread out!

If you don't want to host a party at home, parks and free outdoor play areas are super for summer parties. Plus, there's plenty of open space for children to play some pre-prepared games, as long as you have enough adults to keep an eye on everyone. Take a picnic to keep them well fuelled; why not ask everyone to contribute one item?

If you want to splash out for a special birthday, look into hiring a local space for your child's party. Soft play areas are extremely popular with adventurous kids, although rates may be more expensive during school holidays and weekends, so try to avoid peak times. You can also look into local village halls, which can be hired for a low cost. That way, you don't risk spillages on your carpets!

Themes

A themed party is a great way for kids to dress up or deck the house in decorations. Let them choose the theme and make or buy decorations to match. You can find all sorts of decorations in party shops at a range of prices, and can even tailor your games to suit the theme. Why not have a princess party or a pirate parade? A racing car theme, or afternoon tea party?

You can also make great generic decorations from paper, such as paper chains to hang around the house, or stars and shapes to stick to walls, windows or doors. This is another activity that kids can get involved in, although it might get a bit messy!

A fancy dress party is great fun for kids (and adults!), instead of a theme. If you don't want to splash out on an expensive outfit for your child, there are plenty of websites dedicated to homemade costumes that are cheap and simple to make. Accessories are easy to source, too, for a special finishing touch.

Entertainment

You've sent the invites and prepared the venue, now you need to keep the kids entertained! You can hire professional entertainers to provide the fun, such as clowns, magicians and even actors to play your child's favourite characters. However, there are risks (what if the clown doesn't turn up?) and it's not always a cheap option.

You can also hire bouncy castles for your back garden, which provide hours of fun. It's a good idea to enforce a short bouncy-castle break if you're serving food – you don't want those cocktail sausages resurfacing!

If you're looking for a cheaper option, party games or face painting are easy to prepare and a great way to engage several children at once. Here are some ideas:

Musical chairs

You'll need enough chairs for all the kids participating, minus one! Position them in a circle facing outwards. The kids walk around the chairs to music. When the music stops, they need to sit on a chair – fast! The child left without a seat is out. Remove one seat after each round until a winner is left.

Pass the parcel

A birthday party classic! Here are some ideas for prizes: books, colouring pencils, crayons, craft kits, toys, cards, miniature games or key rings. Make sure the prizes are age appropriate and suitable for all who are taking part.

Pin the tail on the donkey

You can buy a donkey cut-out, or make one yourself! Draw a donkey outline and get your kids to help you colour in with paints, or stick coloured card to your donkey.

Treasure hunt

A great idea for themed parties, especially pirate parties! Hide clues around the house and garden, then send the kids off in groups to search for them. It's always nice to make sure there are enough prizes for everyone, so no one feels left out.

Sleeping lions

This is a fantastic game to calm down excitable young children, if things get out of control! The children lie down on the floor with their eyes closed, pretending to be sleeping lions. Walk around and try to distract the children by talking or tickling. If they move, they are out! The child who stays 'asleep' the longest wins.

There are plenty of games on the Internet for different age groups, if you want something a little more challenging! As for face painting, you can buy cheap paints online or in party stores. Either find some designs on the Internet to copy, or get your best arty friend to come along and help out.

Party bags

Party bags can end up being the most difficult part of a children's party. Little toys soon add up, and often end up lost or broken before they make it home!

Buy a collection of paperback children's books and let the kids choose which to take, or pop them in a little bag with a slice of cake. Books are longer lasting and will be enjoyed over and over again.

Instead of buying plastic party bags, buy brown paper bags and decorate them with your children. You can even fill them with a bag of seeds or a bulb, so they can plant them at home and watch them grow. This is a great eco-friendly gift, with very little cost attached, so you benefit, too.

You can also collect little jars and fill them with goodies; sweets or chocolates always go down well, or how about some little pencil crayons, stickers or craft supplies?

And don't forget the all-important slice of your home-made birthday cake!

Index